POSTCARDS FROM GOD

Imtiaz Dharker was born in Lahore, Pakistan, grew up a Muslim Calvinist in a Lahori household in Glasgow and was adopted by India and married into Wales. She is an accomplished artist and documentary film-maker, and has published five collections with Bloodaxe in Britain, all including her own drawings: *Postcards from god* [including *Purdah*] (1997), *I speak for the devil* (2001), *The terrorist at my table* (2006) *Leaving Fingerprints* (2009) and *Over the Moon* (2014). She was awarded the Queen's Gold Medal for Poetry 2014 for *Over the Moon* and in recognition of a lifetime's commitment to poetry.

IMTIAZ DHARKER

Postcards from god

BLOODAXE BOOKS

First published 1997 by
Bloodaxe Books Ltd,
Eastburn,
South Park,
Hexham,
Northumberland NE46 1BS.

Second impression 2016

www.bloodaxebooks.com
For further information about Bloodaxe titles
please visit our website or write to
the above address for a catalogue.

Supported using public funding by
ARTS COUNCIL
ENGLAND

Cover drawing: Imtiaz Dharker
Author photograph: Ayesha Dharker

Printed in Great Britain by Bell & Bain Limited, Glasgow, Scotland, on
acid-free paper sourced from mills with FSC chain of custody certification.

For Ayesha

ACKNOWLEDGEMENTS

Purdah was first published in India in 1989 by Oxford University Press, Delhi, but without Imtiaz Dharker's drawings, which are published in this edition for the first time. *Postcards from god* was first published in India in 1994 by Viking Penguin. This Bloodaxe edition is the first book to include both sequences.

The author and publishers would like to thank the following people and companies for permission to reproduce the drawings in the book: Jaya and Amitabh Bachchan; Minakshi and Asit Chandmal; Uma and Gerson da Cunha; Shobha and Dilip Dé; Saryu and Vinod Doshi; Chakor Doshi; Sumanto Ghosal; Mala and Harsh Goenka; Kiko Hingorani; Shashi Kapoor; Barota and Jayant Malhoutra; Ismail Merchant; Habiba and Mario Miranda; Bhaichand Patel; Urvi Piramal; S. Rai; Siemens; The Taj Mahal Hotel Bombay.

CONTENTS

Purdah

Postcards from god

BOMBAY: THE NAME OF GOD

Purdah

PURDAH

Purdah I

One day they said
she was old enough to learn some shame.
She found it came quite naturally.

Purdah is a kind of safety.
The body finds a place to hide.
The cloth fans out against the skin
much like the earth that falls
on coffins after they put the dead men in.

People she has known
stand up, sit down as they have always done.
But they make different angles
in the light, their eyes aslant,
a little sly.

She half-remembers things
from someone else's life,
perhaps from yours, or mine –
carefully carrying what we do not own:
between the thighs, a sense of sin.

We sit still, letting the cloth grow
a little closer to our skin.
A light filters inward
through our bodies' walls.
Voices speak inside us,
echoing in the spaces we have just left.

She stands outside herself,
sometimes in all four corners of a room.
Wherever she goes, she is always
inching past herself,
as if she were a clod of earth
and the roots as well,
scratching for a hold
between the first and second rib.

Passing constantly out of her own hands
into the corner of someone else's eyes…
while doors keep opening
inward and again
inward.

Purdah II

The call breaks its back
across the tenements: 'Allah-u-Akbar'.
Your mind throws black shadows
on marble cooled by centuries of dead.
A familiar script racks the walls.
The pages of the Koran
turn, smooth as old bones
in your prodigal hands.
In the tin box of your memory
a coin of comfort rattles
against the strangeness of a foreign land.

* * *

Years of sun were concentrated
into Maulvi's fat dark finger,
hustling across the page,
nudging words into your head;
words unsoiled by sense,
pure rhythm on the tongue.

The body, rocked in time
with twenty others, was lulled
into thinking it had found a home.

* * *

The new Hajji, just fifteen,
had cheeks quite pink with knowledge
and eyes a startling blue.
He snapped a flower off his garland
and looked at you.
There was nothing holy in his look.
Hands that had prayed at Mecca
dropped a sly flower on your Book.

You had been chosen.
Your dreams were full of him for days.
Making pilgrimages to his cheeks,
you were scorched,
long before the judgement,
by the blaze.

Your breasts, still tiny, grew an inch.

* * *

The cracked voice calls again.
A change of place and time.
Much of the colour drains away.
The brightest shades are in your dreams,
a picture-book, a strip of film.
The rest forget to sing.

Evelyn, the medium from Brighton,
said, 'I see you quite different in my head,
not dressed in this cold blue.
I see your mother bringing you
a stretch of brilliant fabric, red.
Yes, crimson red, patterned through
with golden thread.'

There she goes, your mother,
still plotting at your wedding
long after she is dead.

* * *

They have all been sold and bought,
the girls I knew,
unwilling virgins who had been taught,
especially in this strangers' land, to bind
their brightness tightly round,
whatever they might wear,
in the purdah of the mind.

They veiled their eyes
with heavy lids.
They hid their breasts,
but not the fullness of their lips.

* * *

The men you knew
were in your history, striding proud
with heavy feet across a fertile land.

A horde of dead men
held up your head,
above the mean temptations
of those alien hands.
You answered to your race.

Night after virtuous night
you performed for them.
They warmed your bed.

* * *

A coin of comfort in the mosque
clatters down the years of loss.

* * *

You never met those men
with burnt-out eyes, blood
dripping from their beards.
You remember the sun
pouring out of Maulvi's hands.
It was to save the child
the lamb was sacrificed;
to save the man,
the scourge and stones. God was justice.
Justice could be dread.

But woman. Woman,
you have learnt
that when God comes
you hide your head.

* * *

There are so many of me.
I have met them, meet them every day,
recognise their shadows on the streets.
I know their past and future
in the cautious way they place their feet.
I can see behind their veils,
and before they speak
I know their tongues, thick
with the burr of Birmingham
or Leeds.

* * *

Break cover.
Break cover and let us see
the ghosts of the girls with tell-tale lips.
We'll blindfold the spies. Tell me
what you did when the new moon
sliced you out of purdah,
your body shimmering through the lies.

* * *

Saleema of the swan neck
and tragic eyes, knew from films
that the heroine was always pure,
untouched; nevertheless
poured out her breasts to fill the cup
of his white hands
(the mad old artist with the pigeon chest)
and marvelled at her own strange wickedness.

* * *

Bought and sold, and worse,
grown old. She married back home,
as good girls do,
in a flurry of red, the cousin –
hers or mine, I cannot know –
had annual babies, then rebelled at last.

At last a sign, behind the veil,
of life;
found another man, became another wife,
and sank into the mould
of her mother's flesh
and mind, begging approval from the rest.

Her neck is bowed as if she wears a hood.
Eyes still tragic, when you meet her
on the high street,
and watchful as any creature
that lifts its head and sniffs the air
only to scent its own small trail of blood.

* * *

Naseem, you ran away

and your mother burned with shame.
Whatever we did,
the trail was the same:
the tear-stained mother, the gossip aunts
looking for shoots to smother
inside all our cracks.

The table is laden
and you are remembered
among the dead. No going back.
The prayer's said.

And there you are with your English boy
who was going to set you free,
trying to smile and be accepted,
always on your knees.

* * *

There you are, I can see you all now
in the tenements up north.
In or out of purdah. Tied, or bound.

Shaking your box to hear
how freedom rattles...

one coin, one sound.

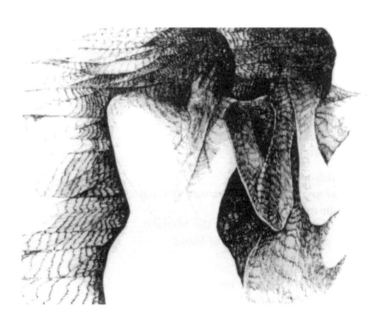

Grace

It is not often
that you come across a place
where you are sure to find
some kind of peace.
The masjid at least, you think.
The grace of light through marble,
a space where fear is filtered out.
Perhaps a patch of ground
where you can at last lay down
your own name, and take another on
a bright mantle
that will fold itself around you:
God the Compassionate, the Merciful.

A wash of marble at your feet.
The man at the door turns
to speak. You look for wisdom,
thinking that is what old men are for.

He does not look at you.
Instead, 'A woman comes
with her eyes concealed.
She trails the month behind her.
We are defiled.'

He rolls his reason on his tongue
and spits it out.
You know again the drought
the blazing eye of faith
can bring about.

'Allah-u-Akbar.'
You say the words to reassure yourself.
Your mouth clears.
God the Compassionate, the Merciful,
created man from clots of blood.

'Bismillah.'
You taste it on your tongue.
Salt, sweet.

A clearing the heart.

Prayer

The place is full of worshippers.
You can tell by the sandals
piled outside, the owners' prints
worn into leather, rubber, plastic,
a picture clearer than their faces
put together, with some originality,
brows and eyes, the slant
of cheek to chin.

What prayer are they whispering?
Each one has left a mark,
the perfect pattern of a need,
sole and heel and toe
in dark curved patches,
heels worn down,
thongs ragged, mended many times.
So many shuffling hopes,
pounded into print,
as clear as the pages of holy books,
illuminated with the glint
of gold around the lettering.

What are they whispering?
Outside, in the sun,
such a quiet crowd
of shoes, thrown together
like a thousand prayers
washing against the walls of God.

Sacrifice

A year of fortune lies
across my neck.
It is promised. It will come,
ripening in its season
under a scheming sun. Sweet
juice will burst through skin
and stain my breast.
There will be no rest
from harvesting.

The blessed touch again
will warm the flesh,
with the season, into fullness
when my year of fortune comes.

I can feel the promise
glinting at my throat.
On the edge of the knife
(prepare the lamb, the goat), sweet
song will burst through skin,
sliced, quite perfectly,
between each remembered sin
and sacrifice,
a saviour thrusting in.

THE HAUNTED HOUSE

Pariah

My shoulders hunch against the cold,
and even more, against their eyes.
It's not that they despise me,
rather that what they see
is inconvenient: I make
an untidy shape
on their street, a scribble leaked
out of a colonial notebook,
somehow indiscreet.

In the winter my breath confronts me
like another enemy,
and the night swoops
snarling at my ears.

My back bends to their voices,
my hands on the ticket,
on the counter, on the thread.
When I must speak to them,
their words take and tie my tongue.
I rarely raise my head.

Their looks are whiplashes.
Perhaps I have transgressed.
But what do they know
of sin and judgement, and
true righteousness?
The skin is a safe boundary
that holds my landscape in,
carried tight against my chest.
Every day I gain
ground: I may live their lies,
but my feet will walk again
on good red soil
through fields of cane
and sunlight delicately laced with flies.

The future leaves a trace
upon the past, and so
I leave my face with them.

In the evening I cleanse my mouth.
There is no help but Allah
and the rituals:
wash the hands to the elbows,
a fluttering of fingertips,
a kind of peace.

The handkerchief tied in corners
on my head, I am prepared.
Over the right shoulder,
flick a prayer.

There
it is – the whiplash
of a familiar pain,
and from my back, the surge
of wings.

White Carnation

Voice I

It didn't matter to me that she was black
I took her on my lap
along with the white carnations I had bought
for the front window, and the two
tins of food for the cat.

She was shy, most of them are.
Quiet little thing, didn't want to talk.
The huge eyes they all have,
accusing you of things
you know you haven't done.

My knees are too old now
to take the weight of children.
The arthritis is bad, but worse
in winter. A tropical July,
this year, with the smell of tar
melting off the roads, and yes,
the scent of strange oils in her hair,
spices rising off her skin. The bus too full,
heat pressing in.

So I must say it was a relief
when she slid off my knees. I called
her back, and gave her a carnation
to make up for all the things
I knew I hadn't done.

Voice II

The bus was a roaring tiger, bellyful
of goats that bleated past me
down the passageway.

At times I am the tiger.
At times the goat.
Usually I smile, to reassure them.

*   *   *

My mother said where
did you get that flower you're late.
Got herself a boyfriend, white, my brother said.

*   *   *

Later at the mirror
I pinned her carnation in my hair,
where it hung, fragrant and crumpled as her skin.

*   *   *

The Haunted House

'Kick the can! Kick the can!
Run!' But don't go near
the haunted house.

Watch you don't, but if you do
slide your back up against the wall,
with your gums chattering in your socks,
you can feel it all...

There are dead women's fingers squirming
out the floor, there are cut-off heads
rolling on the ground, nine hissing arms
wave themselves around, and jelly eyes
are oozing out the door.

'Kick the can! Run!'
When the evenings darkened
and you hid out late
with a clatter from the cans
and your sputtering fears,
through the tenements, down the alleys
that squinted through your eyes
and past your years...

The haunted house could get you,
so that's where you went
because you wanted to be got.
Didn't you, didn't you.

*   *   *

There was nothing like the terror
that you never fought,
that crawled up your legs
when you pressed against the wall
where the dead women groaned;
and at last your breath
grating past your ears
set you apart from the tenement stones.

When you'd stumbled past the coal-bunker
and the leering drunk
and the bodies strangely wagging in the close,
past all the usual shapes of night,
you chose to come
to the place where you stood still
and separate...

a haunted child
knocking at a door.

Going Home

I'll go. But let me close the windows
or the tunnel will come in.
The train nuzzles down the track
that leads back home.
New landscapes spread their legs.

Behind me, with the dregs
of rain, crows clatter in for pickings.
They've made a feast of my going.

On the platform I
could have squatted on patient haunches
among the waiting women
who rake the day with their eyes,
rake the years for a hope of home
as crows comb through the sky.

*　*　*

Fields turn familiar now.
They tug at you between telegraph fingers
that warn you not to stray
from the approved track.
So now you know you're back.

Beyond your tidy groove
the hills arch wanton to the sky.
Even crows rise
into a flight of rain.
Your mind pulls into its station.
Your past climbs in,
puts down its luggage
and looks you in the eyes.

*　*　*

Sometimes there were watermelons
split wide and wedding red,
fragrant,
laughing at the greymouse english day.

* * *

At twelve
'Not a mark on her,
she'll never have an awkward stage'
his wrinkled white hand slipped down her back.

Mummy put me in purdah
or he'll see the hair sprout in my lap.
Mummy put me in purdah quick
or he'll see.

* * *

On the first day of the thirty
days of fasting, the other children
hid beneath the darkest leaves
to eat
soft bread white as their teeth;
giggling with guilt, breath quickening
on a furtive wing of heat.
The bread might have been
a thigh or breast in her mind
gorging on the pride
of first blood warm between her legs.

* * *

Her mind rewinds
the ghazals and punjabi songs.
The camera behind her eyes
watches as she trails
slow-motion chiffon veils; dancing,
she is the heroine
of films that come from home.

The reels spill out bright fields of maize
and a broad, singing man
who flirts with her
through the dingy town.

*   *   *

It was easy to hate, from the tenements,
the ones in the house on the hill.
'They'll come to no good,
daughters higher-educated, mixing
with "belaiti" boys. They'll regret it.'

Yes, they will.
Their heads come rolling down the hill.

*   *   *

Making love. Going home.
Both start with open arms
and a festival spills out.
Your name is scattered,
shattered brightness blinds you
winding round the black holes of your eyes.
Fatelines crack open till the sky
looks through.
Why did you leave?
Why did you come back?
You try to fill the crevices with smiles.
Get down on your knees.
There must be some tenderness
in the splinters of a violent act.

*   *   *

The house lit up.
The door thrown open.
Your dead mother waiting
at the top of the stairs.

*   *   *

I have caged myself inside a stranger's head.

But if you were to open
wide the door, I would not go.
Lovers and forsaken fathers know
the flood will well in them,
find the sun, and dry
to simple stone.

So even when I've tried the world
and found it wanting
tell me
how can I come home?

*   *   *

THE CHILD SINGS

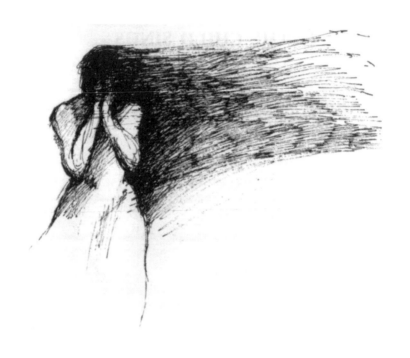

The Child Sings

The child is thinking
nothing.
Sometimes she sings
notes that cannot find
an aim.

*   *   *

Years pass.
And yet it is the same.
She comes back.

A door opens.
Light spills out
around her body,
draped in black.

She is nothing but a crack
where the light forgot to shine.

A Woman's Place

I

Mouths must be watched, especially
if you're a woman. A smile
should be stifled with the sari-end.
No one must see your serenity cracked,
even with delight.

If occasionally you need to scream, do it
alone but in front of a mirror
where you can see the strange shape the mouth makes
before you wipe it off.

II

How can I touch you through
the strangeness of your skin?

All you see is these marks scrawled on paper,
crawled out of the mind's mud,
blinking at the light, mole-blunt
my words.

Can you feel my tongue? There, tunnelling
through the usual mountain of things unsaid;
or the earth's skin splitting
under this year's drought of love?

I pray that I can take your face
just once again between my hands,
and smash, gouge, tear.
Or will it hurt you more
if, very gently, I lay bare
your fear of the skull that lurks
inside your head?

Here I am again, all contact lost. Scratch,
scratch at paper, hoping to draw blood.

III

So far from me, and further.
Our distance is elastic. It grows
upon itself, stretches beyond imagination
till you spring back
through sheer error, the whiplash sting
across the face
reminding us how close we are.
Fear, you tell me, is a woman's place.

Zarina's Mother

It's not that Zarina's mother is callous –
more that she is preoccupied.
There are so many things to do.
Just living is hard enough, when you
have four children,
a drunken husband, and a clawing
hunger tearing you inside.

'Yes, I know what it is she's got.
The doctor told me. Not tomorrow,
not next week, but one day
ten years from now
the disease will flare inside her.'

She stops,
searching for the words to say.
In a place loud with voices
this passes for silence.
Crows rasp, a conversation passed
from throat to throat
and back again.
Beyond the piece of tin
that serves as a door
a pot clatters, a bucket rattles,
a radio plays
songs of love and restlessness.
All this overlays
the sound of water spilled,
sudden squealing children
bathing in the sun.

In this place, everything speaks.
The difficulty is, having spoken,
to be understood.
She lifts her hand
to make a leper's claw.

Zarina looks on, curiously,
then turns away to watch
the other children play.
Six years old.
Still raw, but on the way
to meet her future:
ten years or more.
Not today.

Blessing

The skin cracks like a pod.
There never is enough water.

Imagine the drip of it,
the small splash, echo
in a tin mug,
the voice of a kindly god.

Sometimes, the sudden rush
of fortune. The municipal pipe bursts,
silver crashes to the ground
and the flow has found
a roar of tongues. From the huts,
a congregation: every man woman
child for streets around
butts in, with pots,
brass, copper, aluminium,
plastic buckets,
frantic hands,

and naked children
screaming in the liquid sun,
their highlights polished to perfection,
flashing light,
as the blessing sings
over their small bones.

Another Woman

This morning she bought green 'methi'
in the market, choosing the freshest bunch;
picked up a white radish,
imagined the crunch it would make
between her teeth, the sweet sharp taste,
then put it aside, thinking it
an extravagance; counted her coins
out carefully, tied them, a small bundle
into her sari at the waist;
came home, faced her mother-in-law's
dark looks, took
the leaves and chopped them,
her hands stained yellow from the juice;
cut an onion, fine, and cooked
the whole thing in the pot
(salt and cumin seeds thrown in)
over the stove,
shielding her face from the heat.

The usual words came and beat
their wings against her: the money spent,
curses heaped upon her parents,
who had sent her out
to darken other people's doors.
She crouched, as usual, on the floor
beside the stove.
When the man came home
she did not look into his face
nor raise her head, but bent
her back a little more.
Nothing gave her the right
to speak.

She watched the flame hiss up
and beat against the cheap old pot,
a wing of brightness
against its blackened cheek.

This was the house she had been sent to,
the man she had been bound to,
the future she had been born into.

So when the kerosene was thrown
(just a moment of surprise,
a brilliant spark)
it was the only choice
that she had ever known.

Another torch, blazing in the dark.

Another woman.

We shield our faces from the heat.

Choice

I

I may raise my child in this man's house
or that man's love,
warm her on this one's smile, wean
her to that one's wit,
praise or blame at a chosen moment,
in a considered way, say
yes or no, true, false, tomorrow
not today...

Finally, who will she be
when the choices are made,
when the choosers are dead,
and of the men I love, the teeth are left
chattering with me undergound?
Just the sum of me
and this or that
other?

Who can she be but, helplessly,
herself ?

II

Some day your head won't find my lap
so easily. Trust is a habit you'll soon break.

Once, stroking a kitten's head
throught a haze of fur, I was afraid
of my own hand big and strong and quivering
with the urge to crush.
Here, in the neck's strong curve, the cradling arm,
love leers close to violence.

Your head too fragile, child,
under a mist of hair.

49

Home is this space in my lap, till the body reforms,
tissues stretch, flesh turns firm.
Your kitten-bones will harden,
grow away from me, till you and I are sure
we are both safe.

III

I spent years hiding from your face,
the weight of your arms, warmth
of your breath. Through feverish nights,
dreaming of you, the watchdogs of virtue
and obedience crouched on my chest. 'Shake
them off,' I told myself, and did. Wallowed
in small perversities, celebrated as they came
of age, matured to sins.

I call this freedom now,
watch the word cavort luxuriously, strut
my independence across whole continents
of sheets. But turning from the grasp
of arms, the rasp of breath,
to look through darkened windows at the night,
Mother, I find you staring back at me.

When did my body agree
to wear your face ?

BORDERLINES

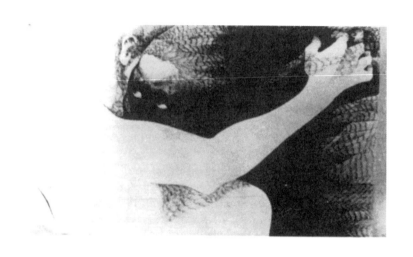

Outline

A solid figure struggles out of rock.
The sculptor's chisel
chose to stop
at just this moment, leaving
the body locked
in a great struggle, trembling
on the fine edge between
being trapped, and being free.

* * *

The artist tries, time after time,
to trap the human body
in a fine outline;
and finds himself, instead, cut loose,
floating free through the spaces
of the wheeling mind.

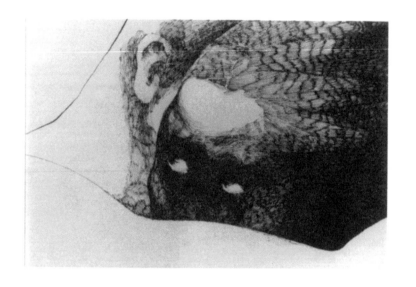

Battle-line

Did you expect dignity?

All you see is bodies
crumpled carelessly, and thrown
away.
The arms and legs are never arranged
heroically.

It's the same with lovers
after the battle-lines are drawn:
combatants thrown
into something they have not
had time to understand.
And in the end, just
a reflex turning away
when there is nothing, really,
left to say;

when the body becomes a territory
shifting across uneasy sheets;

when you retreat behind
the borderline of skin.

Turning, turning,
barbed wire sinking in.

                    *   *   *

These two countries lie
hunched against each other,
distrustful lovers
who have fought bitterly
and turned their backs;
but in sleep, drifted slowly
in, moulding themselves
around the cracks
to fit together,
whole again; at peace.

Forgetful of hostilities
until, in the quiet dawn,
the next attack.

* * *

Checkpoint:
The place in the throat
where words are halted,
not allowed to pass,
where questions form
and are not asked.

Checkpoint:
The space on the skin
that the other cannot touch;
where you are the guard
at every post
holding a deadly host
of secrets in.

Checkpoint:
Another country. You.
Your skin the bright, sharp line
that I must travel to.

* * *

I watch his back,
and from my distance map
its breadth and strength.

His muscles tense.
His body tightens
into a posture of defence.

He goes out, comes in.
His movements are angles
sharp enough to slice my skin.

He cuts across the room
his territory. I watch
the cautious way he turns his head.

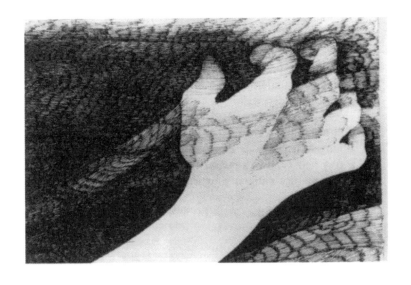

He throws back the sheet. At last
his eyes meet mine.

Together,
we have reached the battle-line.

* * *

Having come home,
all you can do is leave.

Spaces become too small.
Doors and windows begin
to hold your breath.
Floors shift underfoot, you bruise yourself
against a sudden wall.

You come into a room.
Strangers haggle over trivial things,
a grey hair curls in a comb.
Someone tugs sadly at your sleeve.

But no one screams.

* * *

Because, leaving home,
you call yourself free.

Because, behind you,
barbed wire grows
where you once
had planted a tree.

No-man's Land

A bleak view.
A stretch of empty beach
where we once sat;
like chalk across
a blackboard sky, the seagulls screech.

A chill creeps across the sand.
'Is there no way back?' you ask.
I take the words for what they are:
a half-meant signal sent
from no-man's land...

We are countries out of reach.

* * *

Places washed by sea:
places that men may trample,
stamp across with heavy feet,
batter with their bombs
and bullets, shatter
in staccato sound,
still go free.

The victor is behind them,
the gentle wash across the sand,
a rhythm they cannot change,
soothing away their furrows
from the forehead of the earth
with a mother's light, relentless hand.

* * *

It is the women who know
you can take in
the invader, time after time,
and still be whole.

Whether they enter
with loaded guns, or
kind words, you are quite intact.

The fact is, each one
has a borderline
that cannot be erased.

Every borderline becomes a battlefield.

And every night an act of faith.

*   *   *

Here it is again, the border.
Nothing but a piece of ragged land.
Still, some hand has picked you up
on yet another white-hot night
and put you here
(a casual move, part of no great plan)
to stumble across scrub on clumsy feet
surprised, each time, that the demarcation
should be so insignificant.

Under a blazing eye
your shadow shifts, shrinks
back against you.
You stand like some forgotten stone
leaning into a hazed horizon
and wait, again,
for a veil to lift,
certain there is someone you must meet
before it is too late:

the one who never comes.
The face beyond the borderline.

*   *   *

Stone

It won't be long before
you reach that place
where flesh dies gently,
creeping round the bone,
where wisdom lodges in the cracks
that were your eyes.

Without desire, lust, pain,
your face a great, wild landscape
beaten into stone.

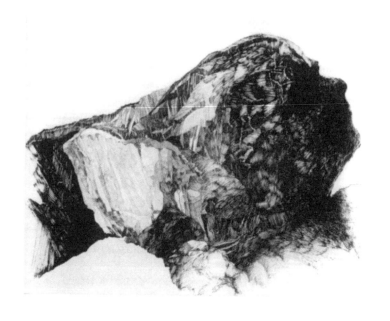

Passage

Your history is a trapdoor
that you must struggle through
blinking from the darkness
into a shower of light.

Exile

A parrot knifes
through the sky's bright skin,
a sting of green.
It takes so little
to make the mind bleed
into another country,

a past that you agreed
to leave behind.

The Word

It is pure power,
not in the throat or on the page
but sliding, coiling and uncoiling   .
in the minds of men
and women, lifting itself to creep
out of their eyes. It slithers
everywhere, over the shoulder,
right or left
prepared to heal or wound,
give birth to a whole nest
of hungry thoughts. This way is madness,
this may change the world, this
tame a thousand beasts, or make monsters
of a million sheep.

And I the keeper, with my
small signs and codes. How long
will it obey my trivial commands? I,
wary of this thing
hissing in its box. A quivering of hands.
It is waiting to be fed,
let loose, one day,
when its moment comes,
upon a world unready
to be stung from sleep.

The Mask

We live with a passion
to destroy, to take and crush and tear,
because for us no one is innocent
and almost innocence is all too rare.
Within each one of us, the scaled beast
lurks, snarling through the cage
of rib on rib, careful construct,
reason and pure sense
that declares us human, and serves,
for now at least, to shield us
from our own consuming rage.

From this, there is no escape.
Power is not always fanged,
smeared with the blood of the lamb.
More often it wears a simpering mask.
More often it looks like us.
Look at us, in that dark mirror.

Our face beginning to take shape.

Image

The picture is complete.
Benign authority strikes a pose,
head up, just the right
suggestion of a smile,
a hint of power around the shoulders,
and the mass of the neck.

The camera will record
it all: the hands' precise movements,
all the correct emphases
captured through an indulgent lens.

You hold so many possibilities
just inside the skin.
You could be any number of things:
manipulator, mechanical pawn,
victim.

The image is never really fixed.
Allow, for one moment, your guard
to slip, and all the world
will catch a glimpse
of the thing you have kept hidden
all this time...

the maggot power
squirming at your eyes.

An Officer's Death

Just before they shot, you sat
quite erect, hands and mouth in place,
eyes on parade.
Your body was contained within
a brittle concept of yourself.

Had this event been just
a name strung up on facts, it might have died
as you lived, closed in upon itself.
But there's the photograph, a screen of grey
on grey, that changes you, quite suddenly:
your pride picked up and thrown away.

Now, an attitude of wonder.
Head thrown back, mouth open, eyes wide.
What god exploded inside your head,
making fierce demands?

What command
let your body loose upon death?

The Rope

Do you think you have buried
your enemy?
Does a man or woman end,
shovelled into the waiting ground
where every creature is a friend,
busy, under a deceptive mound,
with the minute cleaning
and polishing of bones
that grew in the womb,
hardened and prepared themselves
to grasp this state,
quite worked over, smooth
as a pretty stone?

Do you feel, now, you are unbound,
limitations fallen away?
You have found
new power. What a chain
you set in motion,
from thinker into thing.
All that is left of marching
and dissent: these bones knocking
one against the other, gently.

Knocking out a deadly code.
Stones heave slowly, underground.
Ghosts live and breathe
in other minds.
They walk, eat, sleep,
rub up against you
in the street.
They make your future
a bright noose
that hangs above you, swinging
casually, loose,
waiting for the time when you are ready.

The time when even enemies
will come of use.

You see a room
closed up, shutters drawn.
A shadow swinging on a wall...
Somewhere, quietly,
a rope still hanging
above us all.

* * *

One day you hear
he is gone; a hand raised,
head turned, feet
dangling awkwardly above the ground
at that time when motives come
pure and clear,
the still moment before dawn,
before fear.

You hear the sound
of a rope creaking;
a lullaby your grandmother
would sing.
All around you, quite gently,
shadows begin to swing.

Be still, and wait.
You are the cause, the victim
and the one witness:

these are tomorrow's cradles rocking.

Postcards from god

POSTCARDS FROM GOD

Postcards from god I

Yes, I do feel like a visitor,
a tourist in this world
that I once made.
I rarely talk,
except to ask the way,
distrusting my interpreters,
tired out by the babble
of what they do not say.
I walk around through battered streets,
distinctly lost,
looking for landmarks
from another, promised past.

Here, in this strange place,
in a disjointed time,
I am nothing but a space
that someone has to fill.
Images invade me.
Picture postcards overlap my empty face,
demanding to be stamped and sent.

'Dear...'

Who am I speaking to?
I think I may have misplaced the address,
but still, I feel the need
to write to you;
not so much for your sake
as for mine,

to raise these barricades
against my fear:
Postcards from god.
Proof that I was here.

Postcards from god II

My houses turn to palaces,
tuned to satellites, grown vast,
and in their flickering spaces
I am reduced,
my cables lost.

Tossed from room to room,
sound tracks hiss, distorting in my head.
Just outside my mouth are words
I don't believe I said.

Between video walls and my face
is the eye,
made in the inverted image
of the unfinished sky,
a slit where all the unexplained
looks through,
rippled with power, pricked with light.
These are the images I will send to you.

I create the faces
that will belong to you
years from now,
waiting to be lived in, lined,
and put them on postcards
undated to avoid confusing you,
unsigned.

Keep the channels open.
I will keep trying to get through.

Taking the Count

All I am is some kind of dhobi
bow-legged from carrying a bundle
that has always been too big for me.

Every day, I take the count,
I separate the dusters from the sheets,
I beat and rinse and squeeze and pound

till each one is ready to be thrown free,
laid across the ground
under the white-hot critical eye.

Rows of souls washed clean,
all accounted for,
spread out to dry.

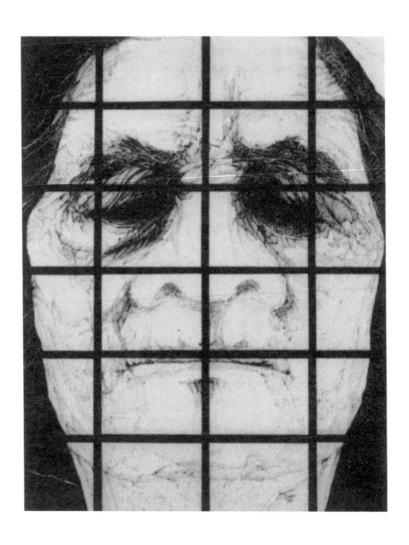

Whim

How did it begin?

Where did my whim start
its journey into this
monstrous, magical thing?

I think I travelled
not outward, but within,
and came back
dragging bits of wreckage
from my dreams:

the ragged cloud, the twisted tree,
a concept of eternity,
a man.

Strange,
to have thought up this thing
in its asymmetry,
no longer an abstraction,
quite complete

from collar-bone to rib to hip,
a length of arm, a fingertip.

What was I thinking of
when I made this?

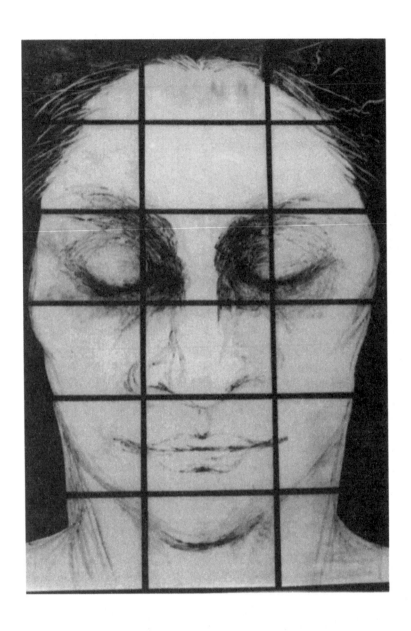

80

Signals

It's too easy for you
to tear me up, throw me away,
take my picture and pull it apart,
sharpen the blade,
cut me out of your heart;

and when it's over you'll say
there was no proof
that I existed anyway.

Was it an accident that I made you?
Do you know what pain it takes
to shake existence out of the million leaves
of creation

every face a pang of birth,
a signal to your spiral brain.

The Line

I could easily smash it all
and start again.

And once it's done
go back to things
whose paths are fixed:
the earth, the moon, the sun.

A child?
It's hard to decide, this time,
where to stop,
how to draw the line.

Pattern

It often happens
that god wears a face you recognise
but do not necessarily like.

The belly curves across
the pattern newly made.

Small hands knock at concave walls.
Five fingers grasp at life.

Wait

Wait, then,
in the bowl of the womb, watching,
mouth gaping, for a bubble
of knowledge, or something
that comes sooner: love.
Shape of belief bright burning
in this rebellious tomb,
howl.
Howl for life, if you have humanity
enough to fear. Do you hear?
Do you dare to breathe
quietly in here, dare to take
this or that uncertain shape?
Wait, then. Open
your undemanding mouth.

It's coming to get you.
The shriek of birth.

The Door

The child screams
at the door of the world.
For a moment, blood runs slow.

Events are waiting for her,
jostling at the gate.

What will she have to show
for this life, waiting to be lived?

I wish I did not have to know.

Aperture

I placed eyes everywhere.
Men added more.
The pupil, dilated,
the open aperture,
the watching lens.

The wound in the forehead,
flashing fire.

These are the organs
of a predatory power.

Words Find Mouths

Things were meant to flow
one from another.
They were meant to grow
into one another; to know
the taste and feel of
being part of one vast whole.

All that stopped
when words found mouths,
when tongues wagged their way
into minds,
and each object shrank, suddenly,
to fit its own precise outline.

You could say
that was when the trouble started:

When things stepped into the cage
of a purpose I must have had
somewhere in my mind.

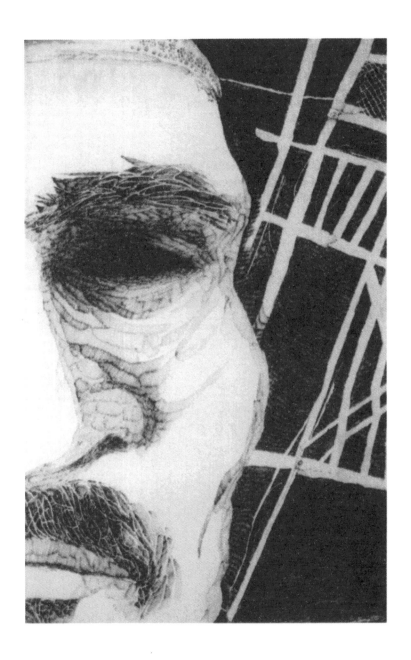

Frame

They have put me in a frame
and left me here
trapped behind glass,
among the hanging clothes
and the smell of yesterday's sweat
to deal with all the demands
that wash up against me.

Can't they see my hands
are tied?

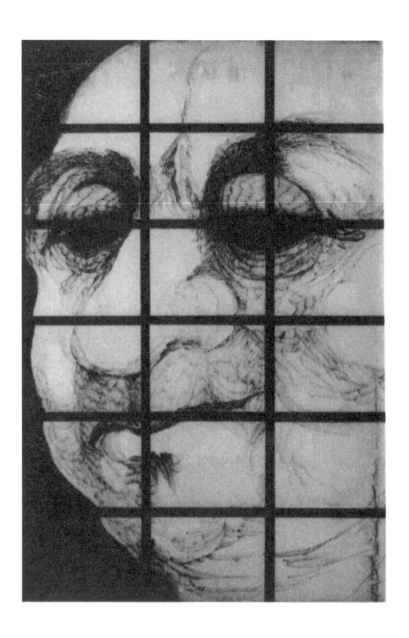

Monsters Grow Out of My Image

My chest opens up,
slashed across with light.
Blood crashes through
inhospitable veins, hammers
at the heart with such
deliberate violence,
the body shivers
like a door just slammed.

Batten your skin against an evil wind.
Rivet your soul.

Everywhere you scream my words,
but you forget my name.

Pulse

What does it all mean?
A space, a wall, a door.
What is there, inside,
that needs protection?

What fingers struggle out of sand,
What nerve wags in the tooth,
What need bursts through
the earth, to blink blindly
at the sun?

The pulse crashes through the head.
Blood beats in a swollen vein,
thrashing against a guarded wall.

Bruises appear, the blow unseen.

Scaffolding

If I were a house
shored up like this
with ancient scaffolding
the threat of bars for windows,
damp roof and door of tin,

would you take the time
to walk into my face,
to move from room to room
and find the quiet space
where I begin?

Would you be tempted
to come in?

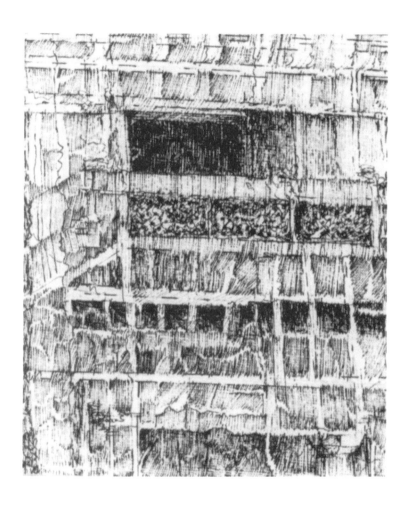

Question 1

I have the biggest remote control
of all. I can channel-hop
and skip and jump
across the world, turning your voices
on and off, start and rewind,
play and stop,
fast forward squeak and double-speak,
murmur mutter mute stammer stutter
gabble rattle rap rasp shout croak
shriek whisper scream chant sing. Nothing.
Static. Snow. White noise.
You're off the air.

Am I there
when I can't hear your voice?

Question 2

Did I create you
in my image

or did you create me
in yours?

Judgement

Yes, a familiar face. I've almost placed you.
It can't be. It is.
You've changed so much. Your hair?
I almost didn't know you.

I didn't want to.
So now we meet for the judgement.
Strange to see you here

in the face of a god
I always knew was you.

All of you! A reunion…
The others too,
whose eyes pierced my back
every time I walked away.

Remember? So much we did together.
So much I did to you.
Now you will take me through
the accusations.
Now you will peel the smiles
in layers off your faces.
Now, beyond expression, we will find
the bone.
Now there's no more running.

I never really was alone.

Prophets in Keds, Under Siege

The world is skidding to an end.
There are strange and precise portents:
god's houses tumble upward.
Shrines burn, stones
and birds plummet from the sky,
hybrid animals sit
in government.

At the pinpoint of the lightning flash
crackling on the railway tracks
at the tip of the crevasse
I'm here at last,
standing at the edge of zero.

I have felt the earth collapse
years below my feet, sweet
sign of the coming judgement day
when we'll shake off
this body like a pod,
and tumble out
to meet you.

Big daddy in the sky,
you never spared the rod,
and the brat next door
grew into a messiah.

In a council flat, our chosen god.
Prophet in keds,
with nothing but salvation
in my head, running to take
the lemming leap
from Disneyland to faith
before the world smashes
like a pot,
I speed out to reach the sea.

I feel the future bend back
a few degrees.
Time is a slippery rope,
coiled to capture me.
Time is certain death,
Okay?

Don't mess with me.

Face

In the most unexpected places
my own face looms up at me.

In a procession on the street,
a jovial elephant head shouts out,
'Hey, don't you know me?
Why are you pretending you can't see?
I am you. You are me.'

On the wall of a mosque, my name
confronts me,
blazed in a passionate calligraphy.

From the dashboard of a taxi, a plastic doll
opens my mouth and speaks.

In a shop, squashed between
detergents and boiled sweets,
my face is painted an unlikely blue
and garlanded with flowers.
My captive eyes smile out at me.

I am a flame, a shining light.
I am crowned with thorns.

Every day, in ways that startle me,
I am reborn.

After Creation

You would think
after all the trouble of Creation,
that things would know their place.

Forget the Garden and the Fall.
Just take all the ordinary things,
the locks and bolts,
the bits of wood,
pieces of tin and plastic,
scraps of food,
the dogs and children,
bicycle wheels,
jars and pots and pumps,
half-pants on a line,

anti-aircraft guns, policemen's
boots and belts, the calendar
full of gods, gas
cylinders, bars of soap.

I had hoped
these things would
work themselves
into some kind of order.

When I began
it was a simpler world.

Things, perhaps, got out of hand.

Living Space

There are just not enough
straight lines. That
is the problem.
Nothing is flat
or parallel. Beams
balance crookedly on supports
thrust off the vertical.
Nails clutch at open seams.
The whole structure leans dangerously
towards the miraculous.

Into this rough frame,
someone has squeezed
a living space

and even dared to place
these eggs in a wire basket,
fragile curves of white
hung out over the dark edge
of a slanted universe,
gathering the light
into themselves,
as if they were
the bright, thin walls of faith.

One Breath

All it would take
is one slammed door
to make the whole thing
fall. One bottle hurled
against a wall,
to start the hammering
on the heart
and crack
the body's shell.
One sneeze, one cough,
one doubt.

All it would take
is one breath,
no more.

Shell

The egg may be
about to hatch
thresholds, windows, floors,
shutters, tiles, a room,
a tulsi plant in a Dalda tin,
mirchi and lemon over the door
to protect the children
fathers mothers brothers two-in-ones.

Stacked one upon the other,
back to back,
tacked on sideways. A place
not private, though it pretends
to walls and bolts;
but battered, cracked
so all the lives show through
the boards and beams
that might as well
be paper, glass.

At last. The promise
of the imperfect shell.

Imprint

This is what happens
when you use left-overs
from other lives, and try
to build with them.

They stare back at you,
knowing they once had
some other purpose,
each piece of corrugated sheet
and wood and plastic
bearing the deep imprint
of alien memories
and puzzlement.

Wedged between the bucket
and the stove,
the gods on postcards find
a rough toe-hold.

Looking around,
they purse their lips
and wonder how they found
themselves here,
confined in one crack
of a hand-me-down world.

They try to remember why they came.

They hammer at their captive images
looking for the memory
that will take them back again.

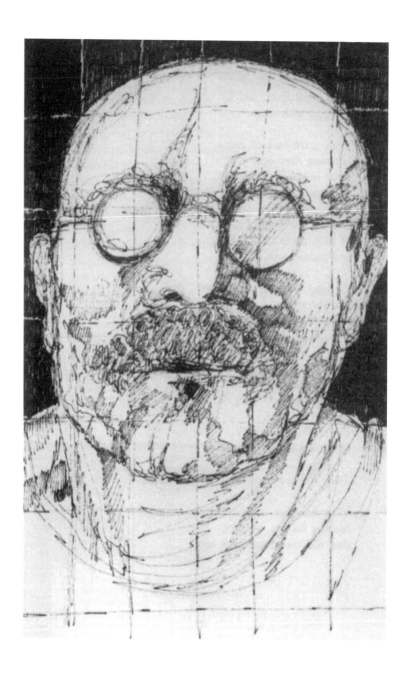

Making Lists

The best way to put
things in order is
to make a list.
The result of this
efficiency is that everything
is named, and given
an allotted place.

But I find, when I begin,
there are too many things,
starting from black holes
all the way to safety pins.

And of course the whole
of history is still there.
Just the fact that it has
already happened doesn't mean
it has gone elsewhere.
It is sitting hunched
on people's backs,
wedged in corners
and in cracks,
and has to be accounted for.
The future too.

But I must admit
the bigger issues interest
me less and less.

My list, as I move down it,
becomes domestic,
a litany of laundry
and of groceries.
These are the things
that preoccupy me.

The woman's blouse is torn.
It is held together
with a safety pin.

In My Image

I watch the woman.
She moves about the cluttered room
her clothes coiled around her,
hissing against her limbs.
Her bangles make small, sharp,
falling sounds.

She measures water carefully from a pot
clinking steel and aluminium.
As she pours, she pours herself.
Her body shifts in her outline,
falling through her own image
into mine.

Within these haphazard walls,
behind the flimsy door,
she becomes something more
than herself,
a bright column
shimmering to the floor,

there, and yet not there.
She is the running stream.
She is the deep well,
the unquiet sea,
the resurrected shore.

Trust

On the taxi and the truck
careening to meet each other
over miles of tar and dust
ride the words
'In God We Trust.'

It acts as a goodluck charm
even when it is phrased
as a command,
or a request,

'Horn please. OK?'
and 'Do not kiss.'

This is the best
that god can do –

hold out a hope
of being singled out and blessed

while men insist
that 'God is Great'
and hurtle optimistically
to meet their fate.

Eggplant

Impossible to hold,
you have to cradle it,
let it slide against your cheek.

If this could speak,
this eggplant,
it would have the voice
of a plump child-god,
purple-blue and sleek
with happiness,
full of milk,
ready to sleep.

The Mark

I contain them all.
The churning blood and heartbeats,
countless souls of men, small animals,
snakes, ants, birds, trees.

They swarm inside me,
insistent as a storm of bees,
clatter across my thoughts,
dragging their futures with them
and their million deaths,
setting down their histories
on the threshold of my tolerance,
laying voice on voice,
familiar as my own,
demanding I think well of them,
begging to come home.

Perhaps I invited this.
I have a memory of a small
white card, stamped with hope;
or was it a woman's body
transparent as a veil
that fell away to reveal
a child curled up,
contained within itself?

And on it, I could half-read,
half-imagine my own scrawl.
'Wish you were here.'

My mark, my will, my need
printed across them all.

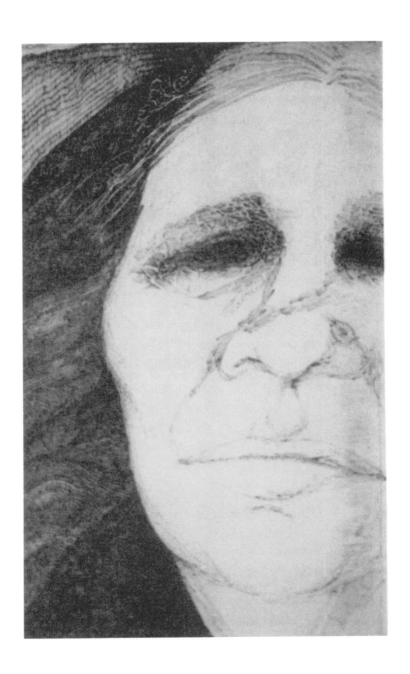

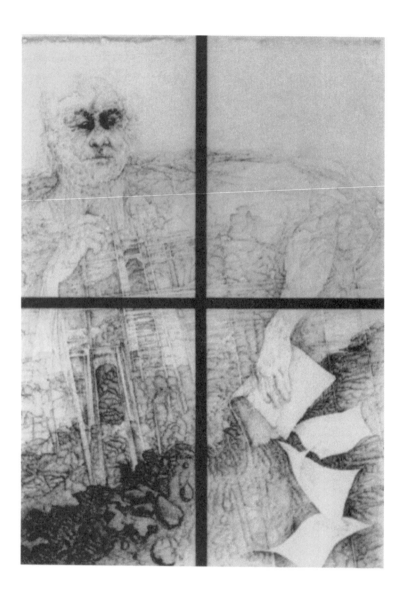

NAMING THE ANGELS

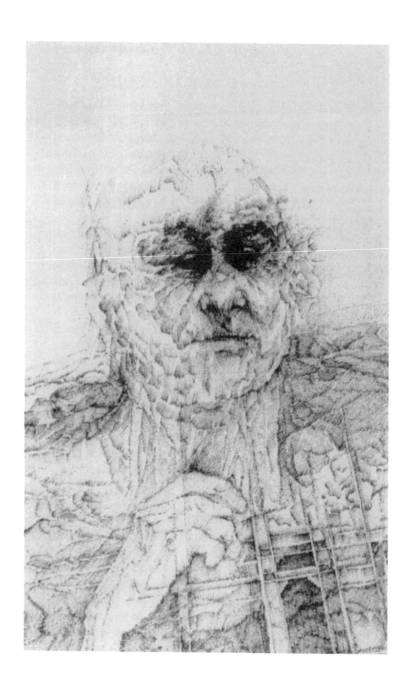

The Key

Yes lord,
we believe in the unseen; we believe
in that which has been
revealed; we need not fear your wrath.
You have not set the seal
upon our hearts, nor concealed
the right path from our eyes,
stopped up our ears, that we
should never hear your word.
We serve you and perceive
the true way. Yours.

But I do not understand:
Those others
who went astray, whose eyes and ears
are locked;
who desire to deceive,
stumbling blindly through the years
towards the judgement day,
illuminated finally by that
great man-fuelled fire,
and no hope of reprieve;

Who turned the key
on them? Who
planned and crafted, turned
the key, burnished with intent,

but you?

Making the Angels

A tumbling of angels:
A frenzy of wings, churning
air, turning the world
on a rare somersault;
sounds stripped bare
on the clatter of stars that spin
against the web of night,
brightness-torn. This
is a time to be born.

This, the maker's moment of play.
'Today,' he says, 'I will make
angels.' And there
they are, triumphant, air-
tossed, a little breathless,
sun trapped in their hair
and wings as they struggle to fly:
A host of fledgling angels, spat
like grape-seed, out
of a newmade, unsuspecting sky.

Naming the Angels

And Adam, when the names
of all the angels flowed
sweet as a prayer upon your tongue,
into a flurry, whisper-wing,
what skies split wide and glowed,
what bells were rung
ice-sharp upon the air?

A hush: each one held his breath
before the word enfolded him, strung
up, suspended there
like beads upon your voice;
and each one bowed,
perhaps to you, perhaps under the great
load of this new knowledge,
the real beginning of the road
from flight to fall.
All of them stung
into separateness.

Alone, within
the pride of being named –
the first sin.

Namesake

Adam, your namesake lives
in Dharavi, ten years old. He
has never faced the angels, survives
with pigs that root
outside the door,
gets up at four,
follows his mother to the hotel
where he helps her cut
the meat and vegetables, washes
it all well, watches
the cooking pots over the stove
and waits, his eyelids drooping,
while behind the wall she sells herself
as often as she can before
they have to hurry home.

He very rarely runs
shrieking with other rain-
splashed children
down the sky-paved lane.

He never turns to look at you.
He has no memory
of the Garden, paradise water
or the Tree.
 But if he did, Adam, he
would not think to blame you
or even me
for the wrath that has been visited,
inexplicably, on him.

Reflected in sheets of water
at his back
stand the avenging angels
he will never see.

Adam's Daughter

Her eye is watchful, twisted
bird-like at me, her mouth
busy at the bread,
teeth frantic at the crust
as small animals
worrying the dead.

At three years old
she has seen enough
to live in dread.
Hands give and often take away.
There is no pattern to it.
The food is there and sometimes
disappears. Her mother's hands
are often kind and suddenly rough,
knowing that the scraps she brings
will never be enough.

And women come
with heavy shoes where feet should be,
stirring up the dust
as crows do, dangerously.
The street worms in upon us,
rubs against her spine.

Her mouth works busily,
but her mind is still,
waiting to see
what my next move will be.
Out of her eyes, I see myself,
crow black, vast,
blocking out the sun.

Adam from New Zealand

Adam is a journalist,
newly arrived in India
at twenty-six, eager to seek
and understand,
and to record it all first-hand.
So on his way into Bombay
he has decided he must see
the real India in Dharavi.

He wants a guided tour,
to be fitted in his schedule
between the film studio
and a visit to the Chor Bazaar.

He doesn't understand
why I refuse to take him,
like all the others, lugging
cameras and microphones,
sunguns, recorders, dictaphones.

How can I serve up Zarina
or her brother Adam
to their random cameras?
They will smile shyly.
The aperture will open
to swallow up their souls.

Their mother will send out
for Thums Up, or
from the stall at the corner of the lane,
glasses of hot, sweet tea.
She will put on a brave face,
but everyone in Dharavi will know
the world has come with cameras
to make a side-show
of her poverty.

And will you come back,
in ten years' time,
with your unidirectional mikes
and your portapacks
to make a record of Zarina's wedding,
or a video of Adam's bride?

Adam, your namesake lives in Dharavi.

But I will keep him out of reach
of your greedy camera.

He is too precious for you to see.

Place

The rock was struck.
And from it gushed twelve springs,
the water heaven-stirred
as childhood is supposed to be,
slipping through the fingers,
sun-struck on the mouth, the face,
each drop shining with the taste
of mercy

and each tribe knew its drinking place.

Perhaps it was nothing but growing older.
Perhaps it was greed
or coming to know too much
that we forgot our place,
birdsong a memory on the mouth.
The sources dried, our people scattered
from innocence to power,
north, west, east, south.

And behind us, the rock
closed in upon itself. Gates
swung shut.

The sun went out.

Your Price

Tell me, what's your price?
What is the price we have to pay
to deliver the children out of evil:
Mangala, two years old,
cast out on the street, betrayed
by her mother, day by day,
not even with a kiss, but just
this, a single crust
given and taken away.
All the children, delivered by mistake;
and those unborn, raked
out of hostile wombs, one mark
between their eyes, the drop of blood
that sang, 'I live' before
they were returned, from mud
to mud.

Deliver our children out of the future
that you have made for them.
There must be some way. Just
say it:

What's your price, lord?

BOMBAY: THE NAME OF GOD

Seats of Power

There is a great shuffling
in the corridors of power,
a flurry of whispering,
a small shower of niceties.
Greetings are exchanged,
hands folded, faces prepared
to give and to receive
the required formalities.
Among such banalities
things go sour.

The old man sits immobile,
only raises an eyebrow
now and then, to flick
a lizard eye around the room.

Speeches are read.
A few points made.
Somewhere else in the city
a blade finds flesh.

Here, in this quiet, civil room
permission has been given
for the carnage to begin.

6 December 1992

This morning I woke
and found my eyelids
turned to glass.
Through closed lids
I saw the whole world
changed to glass.
Glass door, glass lock,
glass gods in makeshift shrines.

When I blink,
glass eyelashes crack.

Outside,
blood runs in transparent veins,
fragile bodies walk the streets.
Through glass clothes
it is clear:

Some are circumcised, some not,
but circumcised or not,
they are all glass.

Glass leaders laugh
and the whole world can see
right through their faces
into their black tongues.

And through the crystal night
the bodies begin to burn.

8 January 1993

The bolt bangs in.
A match is struck and thrown.
The burning has begun.

Afterwards
the bodies are removed
one by one.

And this is left:
blackened saris, trousers, petticoats,
the shell of a television set,
a tin box of bangles
and face cream,
a blistered cupboard
like a looted face
that opened its mouth

in a scream
that never found its end.

1993

We have been bullied into silence.
The things we want are clichés:
Peace and brotherhood,
sanity, the goodness in ourselves.
What kind of words are these
to play with in this age
of fire and blood?

The ugly face is in these days,
crusted with hate and prejudice.
Power has come to roost
in grasping hands.

Monsters stand patiently at our doors,
ringing our bells,
waiting to visit us in our homes.

The beast is upon us,
long arms dangling,

squatting on our shell-bright domes.

The Name of god

I was washing my daughter's hair.
That was when they started
pounding at the door
banging with their sticks, and swords.
Then the fire
spread across the floor.

We ran out through the back,
her hair still wet and full of soap,
past the neighbourhood boys
with hatchets, hacking
out the name of god.

And running, we too breathed the name.
But on our tongues
it did not sound the same.

It had the sound
of children whispering,
water lapping in a pot,
the still flame of an oil-lamp.

The name of god
in my mouth
had a taste I soon forgot.

I think it was the taste
of home.

Absent Without Leave

I

It's easy.
Just step out of your mind,
this way. A little to the left
and there's your body now, cast off,
with the blank look of things
used and left behind.

But catch that head
before it drifts away.
Put it in a box.
Drive down the lid, locked tight
against the sun and rain
and light,
against the fright of many
faces, prying eyes
and poking hands.
Take care of it,
you may want to come back
and pick it up
another day.

II

Your flesh jostles
and rubs against you.
You've turned into a crowd,
too loud to hear itself.

There are your own feet. Up there,
grown magnificent, beyond proportion,
pounding you down,
deeper underground.

And somewhere, you can't
quite place it, you may have found
your mouth, not unfriendly
but a little bored, yawning
in mid-air.

III

Suppose you were to
walk up to the window and
step out?

Would the wind pluck you up
and press you flat upon the sky,
a kite forced to fly
among a scattering of seagulls?

Would you glide or soar
or do anything more
than die?

And first of all,
would you dare
take that one step
into such a crowd of air?

IV

But did I say
these were not my gods?

Small eyes pink with craft,
the china hands of dolls,
plump lips pursed to a flute.
A heavy rope of incense coils
around you. The fat gods
dig you in the ribs and laugh.

Sometimes you hear another god
crackle from a single singer's throat.
Birdflight raises a minar
that goads the sky into smiles.

Distance is not made of miles.

Kite

In the van, the hand
hangs relaxed, rocked
occasionally by the movement
of the wheels over pot-holed roads.

It has an air of being detached
from the things that happened
to the body it belongs to,

or maybe its memory goes further back
beyond the hacking of that
last hour

to a kite launched hopefully
through the air,
unburdened by messages,
just hanging there
with one fine line
holding it to the ground,
above the sagging rooftops
of the shanty town, flung so far
there seemed no need
to look back, or even think
of coming down.

This hand had some skill,
but not the power
to lead, or to manipulate,
or even to defend.

It lifted so late
it is quite untouched.
Over another rut.
It beckons me. I feel
the tug

of the almost invisible line
that stretches from its fingers
all the way to mine.

It draws me in
to the place that I must reach
eventually

down through the rooftops,
down
to the few feet of earth
that shift themselves
and jostle out a space
to fit us underground.

The List

Sudden impact.
The city flies apart,

bits of high-rise apartments,
scraps of slums,
all kinds of shops
empty themselves into the sky.

Loaves of bread explode from bakeries.
Fishes catapult out of the sea.
Buses, suburban trains and taxis
spit out their load.
Things lose their names.

Pieces of wreckage rise
in a slow-motion symmetry.

This must be how war feels:
When ordinary things lose
their sense of gravity.

Old men settle deeper
in their chairs
like sacred stones.
Death is elsewhere.

And then, the last absurdity.
The banging at the door.

You expect more –
perhaps jack-booted men,
not this small crowd
of children, fists
clamped round match-boxes,
sticks and ball-point pens,
and the final weapon:
The list,
to be read aloud.

Your name is there.
It settles on you like a shroud.

Cloth

Rip the faces off those
who look you in the eyes.
Gag the ones who try to speak.
Take their hands and bind them up.
They are nothing, voiceless, weak.

Root out the eyes
that see too much.
Burn the flesh. Break the limbs.
Crumple them between your hands.
Toss the remnants into darkened rooms.

This you can do.
All ease, all liberty
belongs to you.

Oh, and take this too:
A length of cloth.
You may need it.
It could stretch for miles,
and will do
for now at least, to cover up
a few of the bodies
that were inconvenient to you.

But take care –
the fabric's wearing thin
and one day, through the shroud,
their mouths will sprout
and shout aloud.
They will begin to glow,
a shining, shifting crowd.
Their tongues will start to sing.
Their mouths will smile.
Their heads will turn, quite slowly.
Their eyes will burn through yours

and then you too
(who knows?)
may begin to scream,
as they do, for freedom,
for a choice.

Through the muffling cloth
they will be heard

and you will be their chosen voice.

154

Untitled

I wouldn't say I live in this city.
Every day it comes
and collides with me.
I had begun to see
that this daily accident
had its funny side.
Years after I arrived
and after several attempts to leave
I decided to unpack my bags.

The city and I had both survived.
Or so we thought.

This morning I took a breath
or city air
and smelt our death.

This is not an abstraction.
I am trying to tell the truth
in simple words.
At night I turn out of sleep
into the smoke of reality.
It's not Bombay that burns,
but this specific child
screaming behind a bolted door;
this particular man on fire
trapped inside his locked car.

I wish these were imagined things.
I wish I could put them
safely in another poem,
reconcile them with this
paper and this pen
so I could never smell the burning

or hear the breaking glass again.

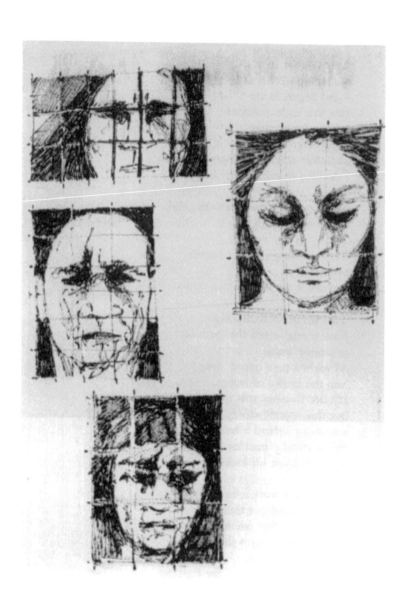

Minority

I was born a foreigner.
I carried on from there
to become a foreigner everywhere
I went, even in the place
planted with my relatives,
six-foot tubers sprouting roots,
their fingers and faces pushing up
new shoots of maize and sugar cane.

All kinds of places and groups
of people who have an admirable
history would, almost certainly,
distance themselves from me.

I don't fit,
like a clumsily-translated poem;

like food cooked in milk of coconut
where you expected ghee or cream,
the unexpected aftertaste
of cardamom or neem.

There's always that point where
the language flips
into an unfamiliar taste;
where words tumble over
a cunning tripwire on the tongue;
where the frame slips,
the reception of an image
not quite tuned, ghost-outlined,
that signals, in their midst,
an alien.

And so I scratch, scratch
through the night, at this
growing scab of black on white.
Everyone has the right
to infiltrate a piece of paper.
A page doesn't fight back.

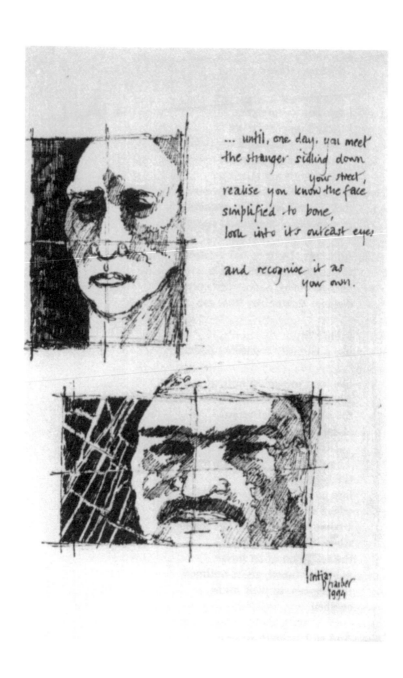

... until, one day, you meet
the stranger sidling down
                 your street,
realise you know the face
simplified to bone,
look into its outcast eyes

and recognise it as
            your own.

And, who knows, these lines
may scratch their way
into your head –
through all the chatter of community,
family, clattering spoons,
children being fed –
immigrate into your bed,
squat in your home,
and in a corner, eat your bread,

until, one day, you meet
the stranger sidling down your street,
realise you know the face
simplified to bone,
look into its outcast eyes
and recognise it as your own.